T0290410

any would be if

any would be if

tanka by norman fischer

chax 2017

Chax Press / PO Box 162 / Victoria, TX 77902

Chax Press is supported in part by the School of
the Arts and Sciences at the University of Houston-
Victoria. We are located in the UHV Center for the
Arts in downtown Victoria, Texas.

Chax acknowledges the support of student interns
and assistants who contribute to our books. In Fall
2016 and Spring 2017 our interns are Gabrielle
DeLao, Sophia Kameitjo, and Julieta Woleslagle.

This book is supported by private donors. We are
thankful to all of our contributors and members.
Please see http://chax.org for more information.

Layout: Jeffrey Higgins

Library of Congress Cataloging-in-Publication Data
Names: Fischer, Norman, 1946- author.
Title: Any would be if : tanka / by Norman Fischer.Description:
Victoria, TX : Chax, 2017. | "A meditative series of poems
that emanate from the author's Zen Buddhist practice."
Identifiers: LCCN 2016052299 | ISBN 9781946104052 (softcover
: acid-free paper)
Classification: LCC PS3556.I763 A6 2017 | DDC 811/.54--dc23
LC record available at https://lccn.loc.gov/2016052299

seepage around toilet's foot

*

traffic jams around toll booth

*

you move in, out, or you see it another way

*

tight words not mine but belong to a place

*

symmetrical depressions where rains fall

*

like I drove buses

*

crunchy paper bag bops couch corner

*

old sweat, peas, peas

*

the day comes out to be something it was

*

punch, or, and, mouth

*

strange, feet in zendo

*

heard, over, herd, herb

*

how hard it's, would be if confident in you

*

8

revise, see again, like, as a method in which to
(shell of)

*

poke terms around too as if at beach

*

I misunderstand you, too

*

subject (goes soft) object (goes off)

*

this one can always be taken out later

*

wise, like this, pull it out

*

She quotes from his or their text

*

can bob, cans bob, bob

*

so I would thus and so could too

*

now this this and this

*

kind of like talking but no

*

whispered so true you too

*

the same is similar

*

experience increases in subtlety and dissolves

*

tiny flies on sneaker toe

*

you hear, from all sides

*

in the words, years, daze

*

merriment to have seen and then to see

*

coupla mice on a stickem trap struggle, stuck

*

something definite like that wall there

*

put the building *inside* and a building all around
it

*

breeze on the tender skin where my wedding
ring usually is

*

this is dynamite

*

several of us authors remained after the plug
was pulled

*

sparrow's head — tiny white skull and feathers,
beak

*

probably vastly exactly

*

look because leap

*

arcs, circles drifts shapes; colonies of amber
light

*

make it up, up to me (you see, or know)

*

every the ideas constitute but fluctuates

*

"one" slashes between "drifting" and "gull"

*

sour societies overdone (a taste for)

*

beauty inside (lost) of **european**

*

poor fucking working stiff

*

in the middle is how things stack up

*

a short gull on *a* tall pole

*

where I was in sun before I am in shade right
now

*

"likewise," he sighed "goodnight"

*

trees deep green, close eyes and

*

over there is where I am

*

endlessly sound, fondly stepping, how over

*

this shirt's too long, so long, like a day or so
later

*

and you (who would) plus (also too) that roars;
all

*

like blocks laid end to end, words as dense

*

force me to, please, that I like

*

if same again, then also different

*

stamped postcard blown again cyclone fence

*

stump: a towers above it

*

no desperate man alone against overwhelming
odds

*

I look out and talk and jump the gap

*

universal haze over the wing

*

lights in the recesses, modernism's bane

*

we are here, twenty minutes is now

*

it coming from; little formica table — death

*

quite a few seats … but people do … even one
then

*

exit, pull emergency, evaluate and integrate

*

you identify the infinite, you name names

*

wisdom … just in time up and down the aisles

*

a little bit of eye and soul is lost

*

simply you in my thoughts a theme

*

larger than one day can be later on

*

lights blinking past the dark: personality

*

you chose that skirt

*

origin of household dirt

*

the door opens so automatically the glass hat

*

only only has that bittersweet tone

*

up the block to the end

*

row after row of windows is the same

*

you who can, that he, and she, would

*

pebbles — things that do

*

this would be too simple yet is so

*

copper leaves, shoeshine: enter one Mr. Mickey
Mouse

*

which represents a reinstatement of in the
woman

*

look at … in the distance which

*

we drove by this way and then than now

*

say this — and the heart the times acknowledge

*

buildings like people in a place

*

these strike me and only just words

*

the mind, like a tear, flows

*

Holy means particular, not like that

*

not stuck literally to what is: bound by
imagination

*

arguing with **aclatter** over

*

telephone silent, angry, cold

*

foreordained destiny's cecity mocks fate

*

buddha claims what you do counts

*

batter up

*

sealant needed around shower

*

skepticism just as doubtful as faith

*

takes your religion, and mines

*

happy rug, players have a good time

*

stuck to reality like glue but which one

*

breathing becomes electric

*

just because is and

*

what we saw seemed

*

hiss of cricket, wrong word

*

now will be then now

*

useful to position anywhere

*

underneath the place where it is here

*

new bookcase seems suitably sturdy

*

everything is some color

*

later on would weather better in climate

*

cars have hair but not here

*

you would condition a moment in that thought

*

I'm the one

*

each sword of grass majestic

*

groups of weeds relate

*

I love is and are is you

*

because of takes the cake over all

*

an over(t) confrontation does it afford you

*

thinking word by word which way

*

being itself is we had a word for it

*

lately firstly latterly is happenstance

*

is is is, what's what's what

*

I think this write that

*

all those books of forgotten pages led to this

*

empty sky a line of people

*

these poems look lonely so small and only

*

literally is the opposite of

*

because there's a missing piece

*

not now, Susan, not now

*

house cracks game ending

*

jam buttresses (*slide! slide!*)

*

light fuses objects eye to eye

*

world just flashes, levels of true

*

a thousand, then thousand of them

*

the castle claims jurisdiction over the sky

*

it's a way to pass the time and say nothing

*

managed to survive without ideal's overthrow
yet

*

buy me a paper

*

does of that (seemingly lose)

*

seeps (such) through crack under door (such)

*

pulls into shape by making virtually no effort

*

caring cares, love loves love

*

to have lived till now, yes and then again

*

one time out breath doesn't get one in

*

jealous, possessive, love you, time short

*

wanted a way to include all

*

in the dome of sky all round

*

houses going up not houses

*

tiniest grasshopper on page

*

I respond to world is me I do

*

crickets hidden and heard

*

patches of sandy places amid grass tufts

*

swirl of cloud behind parallel lines

*

wind moves white spent seedpods

*

feathers from duster jammed into corner

*

not on one mode, mood

*

dials detail decay decidedly

*

not a bad pen at the price

*

this way you can keep it up for what

*

a sentence is an incomplete

*

you always want to find out who done it

*

smack up against it, and so; it's here's
dangerous

*

: left hanging there

*

think if the words not in air as

*

so you foam I understood

*

don't use placenames else you go there

*

cow eat to fly (opposite)

*

nothing outside of out of nothing

*

a way out of much would be too much

*

this true we like

*

peep peep: what next foreseen or out of it
squeezed

*

walk past spirea under cardinal

*

tree fluffs over corner or river

*

big subject hovers over roof beams

*

"eight" is the number you requested

*

the things changed because of the article

*

things assume place names so set the scene

*

at last now's then so this came

*

tufts of grass — onions — spackled shade, the bull

*

hope slows up so you see

*

fence patterns keep from here all that would adorn

*

that that one is already what this one is

*

become the mist is just like asking

*

one and one can play this game two

*

starting up is just like it is, so the fact cry out

*

flowers: all exposed

*

clause beginning, you end

*

thoughts drop one by one like pearls in oil

*

library books upend rows of corn

*

I look at you so what you look at

*

in in would be further, almost out

*

building shakes so cool as therefore or very
building now

*

dreaming, I am that which only a trick would

*

I have one so want more

*

nurses two by two — as if now were stiff

*

and and but but not that

*

Don't want to take one for granted but tops are

*

you would have me if, can't think but for words

*

bees on screen must think flowers there are
crazy too

*

this thing, each one, now another, uses up, our
place here

*

When she spoke bubbles came out of her
mouth

*

fudge was delivered but they lost anyway

*

you pour later on of two in soberly denouncing
the colonel

*

chopped overhead evokes, that the woman, and
now this

*

who can appreciate exactly the fact

*

It's impossible to accord without relation.

*

busy busy busy

*

boy prances penis proud

*

Foot viewed over edge of notebook

*

No words to precisely define at least in this

*

left open wounds would heal

*

insurance plan against

*

favorite telephone or coffee

*

how many ways multiple angles to view room

*

cedar chest taken to college 1906

*

ceanothus in blue room through windowpane

*

mind meets match

*

hail the heart head hand

*

water, anywhere, locked, and so forth

*

this is a project as if it were a ball

*

safe against wit no worries either

*

I would make it in a world unlike this

*

Mother appears in her bed next to her corpse

*

Those are my fingers and have been for years

*

I teach it the way it

*

fans out looking for a supposed plan

*

the chair: the table's twin

*

so if caught it would please; no thanks

*

woke up to excess sour defeat

*

even after all these years government persists

*

the few degraded by the many

*

ka-chunk of door pushing air

*

up speaks to stand on

*

cedar chest manfully under the bird

*

where she is another room should be

*

engaged in sawing it could be a pleasure

*

I want these words just as they are

*

fog hurries in and it is a vacuum

*

full belly tonight and others

*

the letters formed of a sort of cheer

*

so many hours in which nothing conceivable
happens

*

cat purrs into old age

*

they wished hard just to be their

*

I feel so many in a way

*

little by little shades off

*

writing in half sleep visited warmly by words'
destinations

*

this could be anywhere; anytime

*

I'm not moving, will never

*

you went away but no

*

don't waste your breath men

*

take a step in the dark

*

a stretched intensity as "mine"

*

dog's head appears over lap's edge

*

ironing board reclining against jewelry box

*

the several women abut each other the one

*

you comprehend empty the day you leave

*

soft ones be coming

*

a tear for the one one would feel as such

*

rusted wire: how and why

*

gratitude, completeness, characterize religious
life

*

thoughts equivalent at least to this

*

sky shape of peaks, peaks of sky

*

These few words turn on works turn mind
thinks

*

If generations are here it is simply world as it
were

*

spider's web trembles in what wind
momentarily

*

air presses down equally everywhere (un
true)

*

moss, twigs, buds, and and spent seedpods

*

I love verbs to turn world inside out

*

do not forget to urge

*

night comes gradually, career change

*

tiny flies drink at lips, eyes, seek out wet dark
place

*

all the light above

*

so drink if you ...

*

sea of trees

*

now you don't mind but later

*

only one word next

*

little clover tops jerk

*

cumulative effect of numbers, years, tears

*

human, subhuman, inhuman, anti-human,
non-human, humane

*

beaver-chewed snags in channel

*

hair grew back defying the doctors

*

leaning back to drink

*

shit turns white

*

even building tops

*

brown grass nubs in cracks

*

yellow pipe bisects sidewalk

*

bald head above fence post

*

rusted springs in crabgrass

*

newspaper flaps near fence

*

babies being carried

*

buds adorn new trees

*

stacked barrels of various sizes

*

sheet of noisy gray-green tin

*

sheet of blue-gray photographic paper

*

ruined mind spits in face of life's continuing ...
nowhere

*

really an endless road with no destination

*

an old dog-eared pack of lies

*

a beginning would start with this, now

*

in books begin responsibilities

*

chunked rock against quiet sky

*

stationary clouds a hovering hat for peaks

*

flies buzz would be an excuse for consciousness

*

notch in mountains here and beyond

*

never refer to notes, only now is weak

*

shelf of rock, sheltered sage, kids talk

*

I'll wait and weather like this

*

birds' tracks, this is all tracks, evidence

*

she needs me but he and I think of me

*

bread, jam, cream cheese, tea set out for the
meeting

*

leaf lying on a leaf

*

house finch drinks, considers, drinks

*

trayful of peaches on flat rock

*

I am running, late

*

insert key, open garden

*

I remember old camellias in narrow borders
beside old woman's house in Oakland

*

slug trails leads to cigarette butt

*

leaf's complex shadow on sidewalk

*

filing cabinet, thousands of miles of wishes and
propositions

*

stolen words, Yeats, subject of angles

*

write short because mind won't think
consecutive thoughts

*

out of life, as death, would be leaving or coming
home

*

is there any wonder, school's out

*

garden a blot of color

*

might have been a stone, a gopher, "stone" or
"gopher"

*

de Rougemont was right

*

rug stretches forth endlessly, a sea

*

since you have taken my figs I will kick your
mule

*

this is funny but that is not

*

why is a question in a vocabulary

*

these poems may be too self-revealing for com-
fort

*

longing for a point, just here

*

six thieves rob bank of the heart

*

Buddha keeps on talking though you
misunderstand

*

you and that fill the air with sorrow

*

this or that is my point

*

that is over there longingly

*

this closely to have been done

*

if she shows up I'll be damned

*

who is the voice; which speaks

*

this is easy that hard, nearly unbreakable

*

white pages calm as still lake

*

have I already written this one yet

*

unattainable woman sleeps with me nightly

*

re-write that one

*

I cherish

*

singing, sighing, underneath thoughts

*

that you could listen

*

bit apart

*

wife's size taken for granted

*

Grenier lurks just behind the last word

*

so many dishes, dishes, always pots

*

Virginia rail texting in 7th field according to
Larry Silver

*

terms that slide into opposites

*

a shade, left, meaning, so she is gone

*

stones in tumbler so edges smooth

*

this is a metaphor for that

*

only asleep we do

*

mask of the poet crashes into newspaper

*

chairs facing each other empty

*

shout creates silence

*

bridges in the haze

*

one street light left on

*

tire on the abandoned asphalt

*

fire hydrant painted on the street

*

Do Not Enter

*

barbed wire stars

*

pallets piled up

*

Neil hits the first home, pow

*

Looking up form book, grass is greener

*

those frogs' voices almost make me cry

*

pink coffee cup's bitterness

*

would try out ever so tentatively

*

novel in a phrase, whole character study, world

*

6 mat room enough for three people

*

mind won't produce thought, lost

*

body is though, table, gone

*

why let a little thing like death stand between
us

*

first sun over city

*

sounds so intimate when no one home

*

of because never heard

*

they share a past we a present

*

traffic's cars and buses battle

*

you will be rewarded for your pains

*

hands don't touch things

*

drive a stake into ground and don't move

*

things behave accordingly

*

empty wineglass on cluttered desktop

*

lady Buddha wearing pink paper cap

*

sun peeps over hill's edge morning

*

wine fine fear in fear fine wine

*

fire finds further fire

*

these poems would make me famous if only
they and then
*

any would be if
*

yet this yet as continually is
*

these fingers all these years, hands, feet
*

so tap and continue
*

being is so far
*

plentiful conclusions drop
*

I'm not porcine

*

unleavened by consequences and stripped of
fortune

*

seasons call meaning up from there

*

wish would fear just here

*

there's a lot more past than present

*

I'll scream to get your attention to be someone

*

not likely that yet so yet

*

for a way won is lost

*

form pulls you home just there as body is

*

home naturally placed persists so

*

all ever quiet quite the same everywhere

*

size of this book inevitable

*

love them is nothing A, B,

*

curve of rocker leans chair backward

*

pillows, stack of three

*

phone cord meanders across room

*

fragmented possible leanings, none so happier if

*

folded paper a passage into fulcrum world

*

I worry and no reason

*

he said or wrote that and so forth

*

lanterns opted singly — soften

*

there is nothing like that here

*

wanting happens but running towards misery

*

sexual known as wanting to make dark info

*

Jews have survived alterity they are none like
anyway

*

government like pants put on backward

*

half a hat is likely yet half an eye

*

kindness needed amid history's waste

*

if you will supply the rest demand

*

home the place for now

*

presumed coffee, awe combined with intimacy

*

we will adore this flower by any means
necessary

*

you work at so to speak

*

cliff hanger for airplanes atop mountain

*

all that I am is a stomach

*

rude food much to do

*

I am ... oh no

*

work up to the coffee

*

enlist tributaries and meat cynicism with last

*

phone, phoney, not not face to face

*

enliven degenerate blame

*

he is here without flesh

*

where would be a space distinct from time by
human words

*

my mother in law thought my talk contained
pearls of wisdom and food for thought

*

barrel would drain of ink, lungs would empty
air

*

speech proves impediment to speech

*

verb, noun, nounverb, infinitive: to *do*, to *be*,
house, horse

*

canister barrister, canine barroom

*

an old piece of pizza, venerable, out of style,
with tons of character, wisdom, humor, self
possession

*

Three times at the bar look pretty pasty faced
I imagine they come in here every day to sit
secure under the flag of the California Republic.

*

dog's sigh expression centuries of inchoate
oppression

*

is it necessary to eat meat considering the
suffering nearby

*

think not only of your concerns but what is
implied thereby

*

can't catch up to myself beside the delicacy

*

coffee coffee deranged

*

dots would be a novel another way

*

the need to write shoves all else aside as
tractor's scraper

*

Michael operates seeder in the sun, stringy
muscles tight pushing over bumpy ground

*

introspection, heart's answer to sky, clay pot

*

it's only because thinking I am complicates drag
down vines and leaves in front of window

*

so forth go aplenty

*

what was I thinking of after an interval of years

*

this is getting ever older and seeing the plan

*

we cleave through space contains only us and
dark

*

measure, a plus

*

you are not in evidence

*

words cut both ways

*

I invoking no old phrase

*

take boys to basketball, sign up for Little
League, buy ice for soda pop, frown and swoon

*

nose, coffee burn, hopped up and out of synch

*

should end this with a period,

*

crowning, the sage would be a statement

*

you tear forests at last tons of everything

*

weird wind up blows hot blows cold

*

sedge mice in transit through transom

*

little rolled up balls of rag

*

linger in the shower

*

language is a metaphor for

*

none of the truck work

*

pen is a metaphor for meaning it's all right

*

I can only do so many before so many after

*

dog scratches wants in. Dog in.

*

Rilke never washed a dish; saw angels and
fairies in puddles in the mud

*

This is impossible to comprehend

*

you lurk behind constructed corners there are
no corners in space

*

fiery ton — on either side of a rest

*

Listen to each word and **the the** rest will
conform

*

here in the latter — there in the former

*

eventually one will appear twice

*

a pear, appear, perfect

*

last; it shall advance and endure in shoes

*

where will I be when words, worlds, whirl

*

sand sighs after sea recedes

*

tick such an innocent bug to make such trouble
in my arm

*

"Once" there was "a time:" I doubt it

*

period at the end of a sentence

*

purpose of human life should be clarified
eventually

*

Marx did not foresee people as stubborn as
things

*

in just a few sittings

*

mind, meditation, spirit, heart ... very vague

*

in this lonely night never alone for a minute

*

empty, empty: a blade of grass

*

line for line, measure for measure: crickets

*

Aron and Felix may well play in the majors one
day

*

What makes a poem? Intensity

*

it is because of the what space the black
words(they could be white)

*

deranged, elongated — this would mean a lot
elsewhere

*

I wanted prose but stumbled on this

*

Barrett Watten, Ron Silliman, Charles
Bernstein — a rose by my window

*

that I inhibit the reframed universe

*

proceeds by ellipsis

*

let's make a deal in the dell

*

over and over the suspicious that ticks

*

after Reagan, like Jesus

*

the continuous voice even afterward

*

tree in a field toward day's end

*

lapse, lapidary, when wind blows web down

*

inherit capacity for sleep

*

heater sounds like wind on open sea

*

every one of these couldn't be worth keeping

*

wives and husbands knead each other

*

constantly needing to clean

*

our arrangement is such

*

questioned me about that which I know nothing
about

*

very Marin County

*

on my day off

*

I started writing then you continued

*

invented forms of writing never before seen or
since

*

the sewing machine presses up against the
telephone

*

the teacup told us how to hold it

*

I you we must be happy

*

without love no quirks

*

a simple lie so easy goes so far

*

chainsaw growl and dog jumps up to bark

*

bucket of dear laundry

*

life is the preservation of what's left over after

*

with what's ahead we pull ourselves into now
from then

*

so you would reckon it this way

*

cancel the dinner engagement

*

poorly

*

home arrangements can visit fire escape: flat

*

various fits arise but do nothing, you have a
problem

*

happy today would be if you are am adjustment
of stress

*

Eduardo is hopping mad

*

in ½ hour an articulate containment and then
some

*

now it's burning

*

the sound of shovels

*

below a tangle of brush; above a tangle of cloud

*

hills so green, sky so grey, so so so-so

*

cloud, sky, cloud, hill, nothing to say

*

this looks like another place other than

*

now I am higher than the top

*

Power, yes. But power over or for what?

*

Endless projects, tasks, piles of paper, letters
etc.

*

real life ends here

*

looking down on the chicken yard from above

*

what's in the mind floats and dissolves

*

hills to sea as if from before

*

a halo for a tree again

*

projects, to go forward on

*

pen and pencil stand up parallel against wall

*

where is our bright promise now that we
require it?

*

Gary is all restraint

*

long eucalyptus leaves tinkle in breeze

*

forty one years like these

*

such perfect things

*

don't hold me to

*

yes, if read anyway tragically misunderstood

*

I distrust

*

one would mean more since it is less

*

only one one concealed here beneath the many

*

vow then prediction, or vice versa

*

stingy about giving away secrets

*

heater purrs in fits and starts

*

Israelis clamp on what should be released

*

where is this to go from this

*

quoted out of context: the rose

*

O name should obsess for the quiet

*

look slowly powerfully and long

*

if you foresee anything it will be pace

*

warble in the morning bark

*

wellspring, you are a word

*

bird in the marsh, birds pull back
simultaneously

*

there is enough adulation, butter in the cracker

*

yellow in this corner of the garden only

*

form the top a long view

*

it is my opinion that and it is my life which

*

frames stand vertical

*

for passion I would bury or uncover

*

because we're so important love would be a
poison to us

*

don't stop the fight, don't rest a moment

*

a social sense of a person is jargon, dull

*

poets in the poetry wars, shut off the wind, let
out the cat

*

if it doesn't rain the new grass will die

*

sun shafts on book shelves

*

it is meant

*

so forth so

*

to be

*

organized in terms of

*

however is a stop in breath

*

nothing that is not right nothing

*

look at thought, look at things, buffaloed

*

a product of decrease

*

to languish is to follow

*

a tone in a voice

*

chair warm after cat gets up

*

you would be after several years

*

so much faith in so many certainly doubtful

*

identifiable as poems in some way

*

writing that is real things, things that matter as
written

*

the magazines go on. the creek flows to the
ocean

*

always two or three flecks of white lint on the
rug

*

the bucket sloshing soapy dirty water

*

evil is not faced, festered, denied, demoted

*

people *want* to be brutal, need to know about that

*

birdsong automatic with first light

*

eucalyptus flowers — thoughts in the language

*

cat in drawer

*

sun and clouds differ, defer deportment

*

Noah always on first base

*

the books all cancel each other out

*

the hit you need though what's most liked must
have problems

*

played to the hit, hilt, hill or hull (hole, hula)

*

little world bits each would win whole wide
world within

*

diadem, diapason, diaspora

*

South Africa: life depends on public relations

*

to be alive is to be implicated

*

East West evil equal

*

to call an end to strife is to remove a concept

*

shine, bright, crabapple, blossom

*

wide field of deep green grass under hill

*

world grinds on molten skids, floats, crashes,
geologic season

*

Jeffers' poems chill

*

sky to water, impossible to leave

*

coffee from Africa

*

gash in mind equals gash in world

*

(t)here where a wor(l)d was

*

I am the great communicator, no release

*

to be sung to tune of

*

deportment, department, how carry anything
where put it

*

one will come again if teeters, flails

*

listen for typos or topoi

*

along the lines of

*

I'll muddle through I prefer to consider and
consolidate

*

a fortunate mistake in English

*

by the letters, numbers

*

written as "unit"

*

the fact as frightening

*

teacups as breath, tea as desist from collective
bargaining

*

the weary mind worries no more

*

Santoka, Santoka

*

To be in on being to be being is on it

*

Being as being for on or in it as overdetermined

*

To say saying is adventure of tongue

*

new toilet seat neatly installed

*

hammer head head hammer

*

not to speak especially

*

logarhythm

*

to see in the bright day the lack of rain

*

can we afford this can we not

*

I write my talk I talk

*

fly pays a call on eyeball

*

beautiful potatoes

*

to think I am getting paid for this

*

two or three's idea make a lifetime

*

to say one thing now is not the same as saying
that same thing then

*

anything browns, anything burns, something
browns and burns

*

miles and miles of floor

*

sheep shot by sheriff shocks spinster sisters

*

one minute more

*

were this time's final moment this is what I'd
be doing finally

*

it is — that is the end of now must be now

*

not to want to begin unless assured of success

*

a version, a vision of

*

shape, splotch of sunlight on rug near coffee
cup

*

world would compose itself of this and that

*

Jerry doubts language as human chest

*

implicit as trunk lasts

*

it is yet another something to be done

*

can't know how to do this

*

in May there will be May anywhere you go

*

at my age still to be like that

*

mind's finery is this world if mind's eye

*

naturally happier

*

avoiding what must be done is to speak

*

horsehair is what it would have been years ago

*

cat on pile of newspapers on table beside freesia

*

heart's burden sight's divestment

*

little bit of glee in that for me

*

like Chinese food under almost any conditions

*

are these someone else's fingers I've grown
used to

*

Alan's face seemed to be smiling when I entered
— that's impossible

*

the rest is resistance in the end can't say

*

as fast as I can

*

which is the worst thing that can happen

*

fortunately you pass out

*

root beer float at the end of the world, sunset at
the end of the beach

*

what wouldn't work was excised

*

work was extended it yet no territory to push it
into so work floated about the sea

*

frogs pluck into their own feathers over there

*

it would end quietly if at all

*

forest's lips is one lid

*

I *hand* you the fork it over

*

turkey soup would mean turn key shoot or
stoop

*

your boat is on my chin

*

I'll take a picture so see

*

Touch *in* the sense of trees seen they are made
by light

*

mottled branches hand on line response in an
edge of perception or speech

*

Scraps of cloud, shadow, on, above, water

*

huge white mountain round brown eye

*

top trader elastic, concrete, in upside down
world

*

water, water, waiter, would, world, weight,
welter

*

behind the curtain in the light

*

I am searching for frozen never finds it
anywhere, everywhere

*

the she in the scheme wore it is not her

*

I am, like, alive

*

fill up this notebook end this page, water
everywhere

*

Phil Whalen lets begin again with lists

*

Without love there's no sign

*

a blurred photo not as good as the first photo

*

scratch of your pens, ear of the world

*

don't market frozen in the arctic

*

here (first) what is a problem (second) makes a
perfect (third) sentence

*

I'd relax if I were on my way to Japan lately

*

It's not a question about

*

White shoes in instead would weather

*

ran this late would not be in another climate

*

a line or column or pillar of crystal water con-
nects roof to earth

*

white fog confuses hill's edge

*

photos of batters blurred like buildings below
bridge

*

how he did he did OK

*

too high so (throw) it got away (arm) and
scored

*

piano's key a couple ways

*

water not the same as silence, words not water
though water is word

*

interior false exterior prior to knowing

*

photos eventually fade eventually

*

corroborate corporate creeds, willed a world

*

you festers I musters we

*

… hopefully to be taken

*

as many of them as fresh beginnings for

*

Henry James keeps house in lamb and servants

*

infallible doting even-handed moral sense

*

pleasure in peevish conversation no lack of port

*

I'd address to sharp in such later bang or just
call a cab

*

later'd enter before it's time like a lamb past
intrudes on now

*

step in step or step step by step and instep

*

society's what's never useful though people
make a group

*

whose feelings on top of *who*(m)?

*

raven ends

*

lease lend to buy back end

*

ends dusk to begin night

*

late means early only one the other hand

*

foolish like a clock

*

wag bears talk as if progress

*

anything now is visible

*

angelic as ends of spine

*

intoxication means loss of neck

*

who'd him has he not himmed in virtue of her

*

its it, it's it: who

*

neck a mass of itch due to oak

*

never not a real word, nor not real word and nor

*

leave a roof for real, read ends

*

open writing correct, right to turn life

*

life suspect forgetting ends in it

*

summer's sea ear arrives in a river

*

verses rise, versus *toward* words

*

inspection articulation art's worry

*

flurry of fur for rugs

*

grass beats rags, dinnertime

*

constructed in thought as the possible

*

heater's roar, carpeted floor, smooth desktop

*

Silliman just a memory now

*

As time goes by it gets better

*

way or pun would be, then some

*

How in circumstances would I propose to be
just

*

Steven on another continent gives the world
more balance

*

edge of a trailer's roof with bushes above like
hair

*

little light cloud brighter air clue poetry tone

*

day's scope, crisp sun, morning cold, weather
radio, frost on lettuce but amazingly

*

so I got to but lost because

*

take the money out in advance, in out advance

*

last down so don't give up they delivered milk

*

I am still here due to circumstances

*

circumstances tell these things not yet rotted

*

be blind or better kind

*

hold up a last resort at last, least

*

the clip reverberates, I take word as such deep
verbal

*

Charles is so funny because he is omniscient

*

O Buddha great teacher do you have an answer
to this

*

so long as people come they go

*

tabletops gleam in the twilight

*

lit up house on dark hill up there

*

heater rattles, end of world

*

sure touch — words ooze through walls

*

later on little snow would speak like sky

*

talking over table: good to see you

*

driving you ask after death what

*

brown pillow on brown rug next to dresser

*

substantially books

*

cat asleep on pants

*

so easy to be written and be known in that or
not

*

hailstones size of peas littler little porch

*

you are dead I miss you more than before

*

this is read now, now is red

*

I write the text as I own Yosemite National
Park

*

funny telephone is modern times

*

statement of fact stimulates eros

*

Rabbis project when they speak yet no one is
there

*

we sink and swim

*

ordinary, just in case

*

the body a bed and breakfast place

*

grief a threshold of awareness

*

we imagine ourselves and are

*

I love language's crudeness

*

stack of books, be a burden to me

*

carefully pronounced and jumped on

*

spring: garden announces what is meaty in
theory

*

Siberian iris reflection of standard and portable

*

You have good hands

*

I heard it in one era and out of one era

*

bits of fuzz on rug bug's on

*

writing so easy pleasing and inexpensive

*

so that that so was so good and so useful so

*

this is so good and so beautiful

*

wit's bits' to sit on what's shirt you can't get
around

*

so I would think it in peace

*

more writing is entirely recommended to cure it

*

after that there is this from before

*

between you and you this or that

*

placed here it is direct it is traditional
(transitional)

*

bug humor me

*

my shoes alone under sky

*

three red eucalyptus in a row

*

time is wild to put a point to our discussion

*

so your standard diverges from my norm

*

you see me so that I sees you (a mirror)

*

inward (the heart) slowly (temporarily [as if in a place] wants) out

*

forever is only the same poem again

*

downward, sin, aleatory, phlegmatic

*

how deeply she suffered from consciousness

*

careful observation of nature under skylight

*

wanting: wor(l)d rolls forward

*

when by steps or sound (racial, among people)

*

left this part out right

*

walk up so run down

*

alas ah oh hosanna also selah amen

*

midnight frog plops so what then

*

old man with red balloon

*

bunch of big beefy boys blow by

*

it's complete so never rests

*

only one possible like this (is this)

*

one, step, one, a time

*

winter's end, cherry, blossoms, crumpled, hat

*

babies can't taste salt

*

this pain, development, would

*

far way nearly

*

lately deadly dearly nearly

*

nearby there is to wait

*

clam, that slow, not less, tree

*

go back to the beginning

*

back and forth they go, purpose present, yet
hidden

*

what bottoms of shoes do

*

dawn, surprisingly

*

lose sense of time over endless water

*

water and sky meet, smudge, at city's edge

*

clouds are wind if plane would go down

*

"this" would be a systematic wish clearing the
words, sharpening the mind, though I don't
intend it

*

scoreboard flashes under sun

*

confab on mound seen past yellow foul pole

*

kids pour out of stands: "U-RIBE!"

*

overweight umpire on edge of infield grass

*

how hard it would be to hit one of this park

*

napkin airplane soars in complex breeze

*

fans cheer attendance figures

*

green grass littered with players

*

just over that hill: the one one wants one

*

my legs cramp, my head moves its mouth

*

nevertheless, again more

*

it as do be it he me or

*

turn a single letter — it becomes a bird or later

*

someone, anyone, everyone, wondered

*

fragment detachment

*

nature speaks to those who disappear into it

*

olfactory workers on break

*

genus, genius, genous, generous, degenerate,
disingenuous

*

how many meals in a lifetime?

*

sound of someone long gone

*

where there's sentence there's attention

*

wires and beams, stray dog

*

horticulture tour of parlor

*

spent pine needles scattered in cypress tree

*

all those books, lamentation, song, punctuation

*

flat float flout finally

*

self's impossible, listen to rain

*

walking among red leaves looking up ()()()
s k   y

*

car (mind) break down

*

sex in middle age (nice to know you)

*

parts of worlds, words, boxes left unclaimed

*

heron in field tip-toes silent

*

one fixed idea broken

*

foot at end of ankle, hand at wrist

*

(whew! air in air out)

*

translation: pushing the stone aside

*

: mystery image at life's end

*

light wanes but sky's still

*

language shares a common tongue

*

huddled masses with socks

*

arriving in time and late

*

wonder where width went

*

me or it — either way you jump off

*

do get simultaneous animals

*

strip language of emotion, end up with operate

*

predicate, pontificate, travel long distances and
speak truth

*

in a short while craft — not much to do about it

*

a strong pulled out of a word endlessly, never
snaps

*

disabled and detained, probably dispelled

*

place it on a stump

*

all the images my eyes have seen now memory?

*

dumped ashtray on bed when pulled down
covers

*

limited potential so must rely on hope or help

*

Benedict knew God loved him

*

my stupidity, lack of care, laziness, impatience,
all endearing to someone

*

gangrenous tooth defection or flesh
encumbrance

*

acid of sword blade on road of crushed petals

*

rug phrases, race cages

*

aware of trauma in room, mild sinking

*

violin passion on purse derangement

*

Jabès mentions book, desert, God, Jew, nothing

*

mentioning blossoms cements poetic mood

*

insurance reimbursement//worrisome

*

Dr. Laura pins you down

*

taxtrick (who's arbiter of right and wrong)

*

everyone there is dying — you should think of
that

*

long heat of happiness, stiff eyeball

*

wires and beams, stray dog

*

everything brown in the room

*

imitation of poet no longer warm for life

*

catch music: not possible

*

release pit or point ... quiet occurring

*

stone poem about puddles on step

*

red sweater of yesteryear worn, now, worn?

*

career dependency // sky diving // careen and float

*

all stopped " " some light is bright

*

beyond the body limit disturbance

*

wonderful dilemma, icy decisions open into view

*

trees above trimmed bushes, sentinels

*

car (mind) break down

*

long winter's night: distasteful lamplight

*

phone: lost and forgot

*

having a baby, knowing what to do

*

sound of door, voice, wind

*

our house, our house, our house (another's)

*

record, bow, praise, lament, offer, decide, fade

*

no reach

*

fountain and tree attract duck

*

music in the way one goes on

*

where's blend of folk, rhyme's reason

*

one's fixed idea (one is)

*

why not gather, determine (contradiction)

*

who knows interrogative tone, tentative gesture

*

Mexican people see virgin at night

*

turning the bad dead over in the coffin

*

jar in Tennessee (unlikely to be in Memphis)

*

not going to Paris — see it best (tasting name)

*

foot at end of ankle again and still

*

art an end of rankle, sand in fist

*

going slowly one goes further

*

you and I could refer to same

*

pages, like beaches, wet

*

these and those (lips and teeth)

*

which happily family laughter

*

stormy eruption at civilization's end

*

words turning noisy, snarl

*

sprig snapped, a life, crushed blossom

*

Benedict's love, to glide (elision)

*

my disinclinations, thirsty root

*

light wanes but sky's still

*

one repeat (death makes soil)

*

hardy (be slow my heart) tidy

*

which, whither, whether, wither, with, weather,
willy-nilly

*

open mouthclose door**speak**stay warm**

Founded in 1984 in Tucson, Arizona, the mission of Chax is to create community through the publication of books of poetry and related literature that are works of integrity and vision, and through the presentation of poets and other artists in public programs as well as in dialogue with each other in symposia. Chax has published 200 books in a variety of formats, including hand printed letterpress books and chapbooks, hybrid digital and letterpress chapbooks, book arts editions, and trade paperback editions such as the book you are holding. In August 2014 Chax movied to Victoria, Texas, and is presently located in the University of Houston Victoria Center for the Arts.

Recent and in-progress books include *Lizard*, by Sarah Rosenthal, *Dark Ladies*, by Steve McCaffery, *Andalusia*, by Susan Thackrey, *Limerence & Lux*, by Saba Razvi, *Short Course*, by Ted Greenwald & Charles Bernstein, *Diesel Hand*, by Nico Vassilakis, *An Intermittent Music*, by Ted Pearson, *Arrive on Wave: Collected Poems*, by Gil Ott, *What We Do: Essays for Poets*, by Michael Gottlieb, *Autocinema*, by Gaspar Orozco, *The Letters of Carla, the letter b*, by Benjamin Hollander, and several other books to come.

You may find CHAX online at *http://chax.org*